Editor
Eric Migliaccio

Contributing Editor
Wanda Kelly

Managing Editor
Ina Massler Levin, M.A.

Editor-in-Chief
Sharon Coan, M.S. Ed.

Cover Artist
Barb Lorseyedi

Art Coordinator
Kevin Barnes

Imaging
James Edward Grace
Temo Parra

Product Manager
Phil Garcia

Publisher
Mary D. Smith, M.S. Ed.

P9-CER-595

Practice Makes Perfect

Writing Paragraphs

GRADE 4

Author

Wanda Kelly

Teacher Created Resources

Teacher Created Resources, Inc.
6421 Industry Way
Westminster, CA 92683
www.teachercreated.com
ISBN-0-7439-3343-5
©*2002 Teacher Created Resources, Inc.*
Reprinted, 2005
Made in U.S.A.

Table of Contents

Introduction 3

Section 1: Review the Basics

Sentences 4

Capitalization 5

Punctuation 6

Spelling 7

Assessment: The Basics 8

Section 2: Plan a Paragraph

Choose a Topic and List Ideas 10

Paragraph Planner 11

Put Ideas in Order 12

Develop Sentences with Transitions 13

Section 3: Develop a Paragraph

Beginning: Topic Sentence 14

Middle: Body Sentences 15

End: Concluding Sentence 16

Assessment: Develop a Paragraph 17

Section 4: Revise and Edit a Paragraph

Specific Details 18

Sentence Structure 19

Word Choice 20

Figurative Language 22

Tone 24

Assessment: Revise and Edit a Paragraph 25

Section 5: Proofread a Paragraph

Check Grammar, Capitalization, Punctuation, Spelling 27

Paragraph Checklist 28

Section 6: Write a Paragraph

Descriptions of Paragraphs and Sample Topics 29

Write an Expository Paragraph 30

Write a Narrative Paragraph 32

Write an Autobiographical Paragraph 34

Write a Friendly Letter 36

Section 7: Write an Essay

Description of an Essay and Sample Topics 38

Choose an Essay Topic and List Ideas 40

Essay Outline 41

Develop Essay Paragraphs 42

Revise, Edit, and Proofread the Essay 45

Section 8: Unit Assessment 46

Answer Key 48

Introduction

The old adage "practice makes perfect" can really hold true for your child and his or her education. The more your child has practice with and exposure to concepts being taught in school, the more success he or she is likely to find. For many parents, knowing how to help their children may be frustrating because the resources may not be readily available.

As a parent, it is also difficult to know where to focus your efforts so that the extra practice your child receives at home supports what he or she is learning in school.

This book has been written to help parents and teachers reinforce basic skills with children. *Practice Makes Perfect: Writing Paragraphs* reviews basic composition skills for fourth graders. The exercises in this book can be done sequentially or can be taken out of order, as needed.

The following standards or objectives will be met or reinforced by completing the practice pages included in this book. These standards and objectives are similar to the ones required by your state and school district because they are considered appropriate for fourth graders.

- The student is familiar with the basic rules of capitalization, punctuation, and spelling as well as able to identify and write complete sentences.

- The student is able to plan a paragraph before beginning to write (choose a topic and organize ideas).

- The student can develop a paragraph with a beginning, middle, and end.

- The student can revise and edit a paragraph—use specific details, vary sentence structure, improve word choice, use figurative language, communicate a coherent tone, and maintain a consistent voice throughout the paragraph.

- The student can proofread a paragraph by checking grammar, capitalization, punctuation, and spelling.

- The student can write paragraphs that explain, tell stories, relate personal experiences, compare and contrast, persuade and/or express opinions, and that are letters to friends.

- The student can write a three-paragraph essay based on the planning and development models used for paragraph writing.

How to Make the Most of This Book

Here are some useful ideas for making the most of this book:

- Set aside a specific place in your home to work on this book. Keep it neat and tidy, with the necessary materials on hand.

- Set up a certain time of day to work on these practice pages to establish consistency; or look for times in your day or week that are less hectic and more conducive to practicing skills.

- Keep all practice sessions with your child positive and constructive. If your child becomes frustrated or tense, set the book aside and look for another time to practice.

- Review the work your child has done.

- Pay attention to the areas in which your child has the most difficulty. Provide extra guidance and exercises in those areas.

Sentences

There are four kinds of sentences: declarative, interrogative, imperative, and exclamatory.

♦ A *declarative sentence* makes a statement and ends with a period.

♦ An *interrogative sentence* asks a question and ends with a question mark.

♦ An *imperative sentence* makes a command and ends with a period.

♦ An *exclamatory sentence* shows a strong emotion and ends with an exclamation point.

1. Write a *declarative sentence* about your best friend._____

    _____

2. Write an *interrogative sentence* that is addressed to your teacher._____

    _____

3. Write an *imperative sentence* that is directed to someone who is irritating you._____

    _____

4. Write an *exclamatory sentence* that expresses your feeling about winning a prize. _____

    _____

Change the following sentence fragments into complete sentences. Write any run-on sentences as two separate sentences.

5. I like to go camping the last time we went, we saw a bear._____

    _____

    _____

6. Went flying in the air. _____

7. Ran into the street._____

8. Watch out for the slippery ice you could fall and hurt yourself. _____

    _____

    _____

Capitalization

Among those words that should be capitalized are the following:

♦ the first word of a sentence
♦ proper nouns
♦ the pronoun "I"
♦ titles and names of clubs, businesses, and organizations
♦ months, days, holidays, historical events
♦ main words in media titles (not prepositions, conjunctions, or articles that aren't the first words)

Write on the lines the words that should be capitalized in the following sentences.

1. the eiffel tower is located in paris, france. _____

   _____

2. edgar allan poe wrote the thrilling short story "the fall of the house of usher." _____

   _____

3. the novel *the castle in the attic* is an adventure story based on the middle ages. _____

   _____

4. i am going to receive the magazine *car and driver* on the first tuesday in march. _____

   _____

5. the statue of liberty, a gift to the united states from france, is visible from new york city. ___

   _____

6. did you see the thanksgiving day parade as it proceeded down fifth avenue? _____

   _____

7. the taj mahal, an indian tomb, is an example of the blending of hindu and muslim architecture. _____

   _____

8. *the nutcracker*, a famous ballet, is performed during the christmas season._____

   _____

9. i told dr. hutchison that i was not ill enough to be admitted to oakwood hospital in best, texas. _____

   _____

Punctuation

♦ Commas separate words and phrases in a series; separate city and state; and separate introductory words, phrases, and clauses from the rest of the sentence.

♦ Commas and coordinating conjunctions (and, or, but) join complete sentences.

♦ Apostrophes are used in contractions and with nouns and pronouns to show possession.

♦ Quotation marks are used for direct speech.

Add the correct punctuation when you rewrite the following sentences.

1. Please give our guest a warm welcome said the host of the talk show. _____

   _____

2. Governor how will the new tax increase affect the local schools asked the reporter. _____

   _____

   _____

3. Be careful driving to work warned the meteorologist. Freezing temperatures have caused black ice to form on the highways. _____

   _____

4. Mars Jupiter Venus and Saturn are planets in our solar system. _____

   _____

5. The babys tears wouldnt stop for hours. _____

   _____

6. The *Titanic* sank in the Atlantic Ocean on April 15 1912 and there were relatively few survivors of that awful night._____

   _____

7. Flour eggs and cheese are on the shopping list but I dont know when Im going to the store.

   _____

   _____

Spelling

Write on the line the correct spelling of the word according to the way it is used in the sentence.

1. _____ (**Where, Wear**) are you going this afternoon?

2. _____ (**There, Their, They're**) are _____ (**eight, ate**) students absent.

3. John broke his _____ (**tow, toe**) while skateboarding.

4. The youngster has _____ (**groan, grown**) three inches this year.

5. _____ (**Would, wood**) you like to spend this weekend in Florida?

6. _____ (**Too, To, Two**) many ships have been lost at _____ (**see, sea**).

7. Who will play the _____ (**roll, role**) of the _____ (**witch, which**)?

8. Do you _____ (**hear, here**) the _____ (**planes, plains**) approach?

9. The _____ (**road, rode**) leading to the _____ (**steel, steal**) mill is closed.

10. Do you _____ (**know, no**) how to _____ (**sew, so**) a seam?

Find the misspelled words in the paragraph and spell them correctly on the lines below.

11. One day the forth-graid class went on a tripp too the zoo. They took a bus to get their.

   _____

12. Evryone formed groops to ture the zoo. The blew groop went to sea the bares, the read

   _____

13. groop went to the seels, and the yelow groop wawked to the monkie area. At nune, the

   _____

14. groops met for lunch. The children eight sandwitches and drank watir. Aftar lunch

   _____

15. they saw a burd show in the zoo theeter. When the show was ovur, it was thime to go.

   _____

Assessment: The Basics

Write responses to the following sentences by using the kinds of sentences listed.

1. I would like to go to Jamaica for my vacation. (**interrogative**) _____
   _____

2. You have just discovered red spots all over your body. (**exclamatory**) _____
   _____

3. You want your little brother to follow your instructions. (**imperative**) _____
   _____

4. Do you think you will always live in the same state? (**declarative**) _____
   _____

5. You cannot find the money your grandparents gave you for Christmas.

   (interrogative sentence) _____
   _____

   (imperative sentence) _____
   _____

   (declarative sentence) _____
   _____

   (exclamatory sentence) _____
   _____

6. You have just learned that some important guests are coming to your home, and your room, which they will want to see, is a disaster area.

   (interrogative sentence) _____
   _____

   (imperative sentence) _____
   _____

   (declarative sentence) _____
   _____

   (exclamatory sentence) _____
   _____

Assessment: The Basics *(cont.)*

Correct the capitalization, punctuation, and spelling when you rewrite the paragraph below.

I went to the store because I needed to get something for lunch my stomach was growling so much that a little boy sitting in a shopping cart could hear it Mom he said he has a rumbly tumbly shush said his mother I turned to the little boy and asked I have a what A rumbly tumbly he said and smile shyly. A rumbly tumbly, a rumbly tumbly I said over and over again the little boy started to giggle and I was even hungrier than before yikes I said to the little boy. I have to get something to eat before my rumbly tumbly tumbles the little boy stopped giggling pointed his finger at me and said go get something to eat right now before your rumbly tumbly tumbles okay I said as I rushed down the aisle toward the apples and bananas.

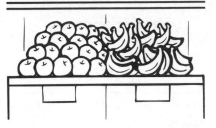

_____

_____

_____

_____

_____

_____

_____

_____

Choose a Topic and List Ideas

A paragraph should be about a single, narrow topic. After you choose a topic, you make a list of ideas or details to use when writing about that topic.

In the box is a list of six topics about which you might choose to write. Below the box are six idea lists. First, write the correct topic above each list of ideas or details. Then add one idea to each list.

good friends	**Thanksgiving**	**pets**
movies	**wintertime**	**exercise**

1. **Topic:** _____

   - a time family comes together
   - most delicious meal of the year
   - reminder of how fortunate we are
   - _____

2. **Topic:** _____

   - like adventure best of all
   - don't like mushy romances
   - prefer to go to matinees
   - _____

3. **Topic:** _____

   - favorite pastime is skiing
   - also like to go ice skating
   - inside, reading by the fire
   - _____

4. **Topic:** _____

   - keeps a secret
   - goes camping with me
   - lets me borrow clothes
   - _____

5. **Topic:** _____

   - favorite is walking
   - jogging hard on my knees
   - prefer to be outside
   - _____

6. **Topic:** _____

   - teach responsibility
   - reward owner with love
   - dog is the best
   - _____

Paragraph Planner

Use this paragraph planner to help plan and organize your ideas for a paragraph. Choose a topic from page 10—or any other subject you would like to write a short paragraph about.

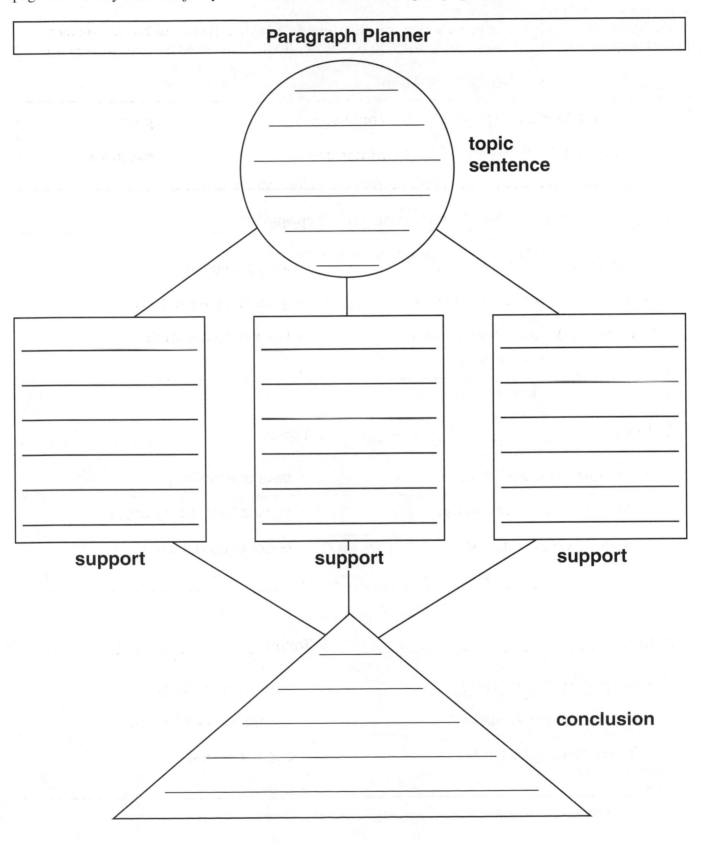

Paragraph Planner

topic
sentence

support   support   support

conclusion

Put Ideas in Order

After you have your topic and at least three main ideas, you need to decide the order of the ideas or supporting details. One basic kind of organization is *chronological order*, or order according to time— what happened first, second, third, etc.

Put these ideas into chronological order by numbering them from first (1) to last (9).

_____ list of supporting details

_____ compose title

_____ decide on idea for topic

_____ develop list of details into sentences for body of paragraph

_____ organize list of details (time, space, similarities)

_____ write first copy of paragraph (beginning, middle, end)

_____ proof and edit paragraph

_____ develop topic sentence

_____ develop concluding sentence

Next, use the list above to write a paragraph. Put each item in the form of a sentence and use the order you decided on.

_____

_____

_____

_____

_____

_____

_____

_____

_____

Develop Sentences with Transitions

If you have not already done so, give your paragraph a title. Proofread it, checking for grammar, capitalization, punctuation, and spelling errors. Also check for fragments and run-on sentences.

Rewrite your paragraph, using some of the words in the box to build bridges from sentence to sentence.

finally	next	then	in addition	also
last	as	when	another	however
first	second	third	after that	furthermore

_____

_____

_____

_____

_____

_____

_____

_____

_____

_____

Beginning: Topic Sentence

The topic sentence is the guide for the rest of the paragraph. It lets the reader know exactly what the paragraph is about. Every detail used must refer to the content of the topic sentence.

♦ Create a topic sentence for each main idea or topic below.

♦ Two spaces have been left blank so that you can write your own topics and the topic sentences to go with them.

1. school band

   _____

2. my neighborhood

   _____

3. my family

   _____

4. spring

   _____

5. importance of music

   _____

6. best vacation spot

   _____

7. computer uses

   _____

8. _____

   _____

9. _____

   _____

14

Middle: Body Sentences

Body sentences or supporting details expand the topic sentence. They help make the topic or main idea clearer and give significant information about it.

- ♦ Choose one of the topics from the previous page, one you added, or one of the others, for which you can develop supporting details.

- ♦ Write the topic sentence.

- ♦ On the lines below the topic sentence, write at least six sentences that are details that give specific information about your topic sentence. (Your choice of topic will be decided by the number of supporting details you can think of.)

topic sentence

_____

_____

body sentences

_____

_____

_____

_____

_____

_____

_____

End: Concluding Sentence

The final sentence of a paragraph is the closing or concluding sentence. It comes at the end of the supporting details or the body of the paragraph. The conclusion should express the feeling, attitude, or point of the paragraph.

Add concluding sentences to the following paragraphs.

My family's new house is a very comfortable place to be. One thing that makes it so comfortable is that I now have a room of my own and do not have to share with my messy younger brother. Another thing is that the temperature is more even because of the new construction. Best of all, we now have a kitchen that is big enough for a table and chairs, so we can have our family meals. That means I usually don't have to worry about spilling things on the dining room carpet when I eat.

concluding sentence: _____

_____

Geraldine, my older sister, can be a really big nuisance. Her main fault is that she cannot mind her own business. If one of my friends comes to visit for the afternoon or to stay overnight, we never have any privacy. For some reason, Geraldine seems to think that she should supervise us. That means that, if we are sitting in my room listening to music or watching television, she will come in without being asked and check to see, I guess, that we are not doing anything that she thinks we should not be doing.

concluding sentence: _____

_____

Assessment: Develop a Paragraph

♦ Add a conclusion to the topic sentence and body sentences that you composed on page 15.

♦ Write the complete paragraph below.

♦ Add a title that is based on the content of the topic sentence of your paragraph.

_____

_____

_____

_____

_____

_____

_____

_____

_____

_____

_____

_____

Specific Details

On the lines below, list the details that do not support the topic sentence of this paragraph.

Camping Is Fun

Camping is fun for many reasons. It is fun to be out in the country, far away from the cares of everyday life. I don't have to worry about things like chores and homework. I got a good grade on my last homework assignment, though. Even though there are camping chores I must do, somehow they are duties I look forward to. Last week at school I had hall duty. I enjoy building a campfire and keeping it going. Our home fireplace uses gas. If we are camping near a lake or stream, I can go fishing, one of my favorite pastimes. I can't remember whether I put plenty of food in my fish tank at home. There is nothing better than freshly caught fish cooked over an open campfire. My mother says that the fish at our local market do not always seem fresh to her. Yes, give me a camp in the woods, a roaring campfire, and fish to catch and eat, and I am truly a happy camper.

_____

_____

_____

_____

_____

_____

_____

_____

Sentence Structure

One way to improve the quality of your paragraphs is to combine short, simple sentences.

Example: Jarrod was beside us. Jake was beside us. We did not know they were even in the house.

Jarrod and Jake were beside us before we knew they were even in the house.

Another way to make your sentences more interesting is to move around the parts of your sentences so they do not always start the same way, with the subject, for example.

Example: Before we knew they were even in the house, Jarrod and Jake were beside us.

Improve the sentences in the following paragraph by combining short, simple ones and by moving around the parts of the sentences so they do not always start the same way. (You may also change the order of the sentences and add or remove specific details.)

Trees Bear Gifts

Trees give us many things. Trees give us shade on hot days. Trees give us wood with which to build our homes. Trees give us fruit to eat. Trees give us leaves we can use for mulch. Trees provide shelter for the birds and other animals we enjoy. Trees give shelter from the rain. Trees can be good places to hide in. Trees can be good places to play in. Trees give us a place to build tree houses. Trees are also beautiful to look at. Trees may stay green all year long. Trees may lose all their leaves in the fall and winter. Trees may produce flowers.

_____

_____

_____

_____

_____

_____

Word Choice

Nouns

Substitute exact or more specific nouns for the vague or general nouns in italics.

> *Example:* That *thing* was horrid. That *spider* was horrid.

1. Jolene played with her dolls for a *time*. _____

   _____

2. The *music* was enjoyable. _____

   _____

3. They visited that historic *building*. _____

   _____

4. My father put the *objects* together._____

   _____

5. My mother added *ingredients* to her recipe. _____

   _____

Verbs

Substitute exact or more vivid verbs for the vague verbs in italics.

> *Example:* Jolene *walked* home. Jolene *skipped* home.

1. Arvid *ran* all the way home. _____

   _____

2. Jerry *thinks* Jane is nice. _____

   _____

3. The quarterback *threw* the football.

   _____

4. My mother *spoke* to me three times. _____

   _____

. 5. Louise *ate* three hamburgers. _____

   _____

Word Choice *(cont.)*

Adjectives

In addition to using the noun substitutes you made on the previous page, add exact adjectives to describe them.

    Example: That *gigantic spider* was horrid.

1. Jolene played with her dolls for a *time.* _____

    _____

2. The *music* was enjoyable. _____

    _____

3. They visited that historic *building.* _____

    _____

4. My father put the *objects* together._____

    _____

5. My mother added *ingredients* to her recipe. _____

    _____

Adverbs

In addition to using the verb substitutes you made on the previous page, add exact adverbs to describe them.

    Example: Jolene *cheerfully* skipped home.

1. Arvid *ran* all the way home. _____

    _____

2. Jerry *thinks* Jane is nice. _____

    _____

3. The quarterback *threw* the football. _____

    _____

4. My mother *spoke* to me three times. _____

    _____

5. Louise *ate* three hamburgers. _____

    _____

Figurative Language

Similes

A *simile* is a direct comparison between two unrelated things indicating a likeness that exists in one special way. A simile uses *like* or *as* to make the comparison.

  Example: Jerrod swims *like a fish*.

Use the following to create similes. You may add more than one word.

1. The fence is as rickety as _____

2. The clerk is as mean as _____

3. The fish is as slippery as_____

4. The airplane flies as high as _____

5. The groan was as loud as _____

6. The tiger runs like a_____

7. The clouds were as black as _____

8. The cold was as_____

9. The spring flowers looked like _____

10. The boy leaped like a_____

Create similes of your own to describe the following:

11. a formation of clouds in the sky

_____

12. a big, black crow

_____

13. the way you feel just before you dive

_____

14. a hummingbird at a feeder

_____

15. your angry friend

_____

Figurative Language *(cont.)*

Metaphors

A metaphor is an indirect comparison between two unrelated things, indicating a likeness that exists in one special way. A metaphor does not use *like* or *as* to make its comparison. A metaphor states one thing acts like or appears to be another.

Example: Justin is a pig at the table. (*simile:* Justin eats like a pig.)

Use the following to create metaphors. You may add more than one word.

1. The child's wagon is_____

2. The kitten is _____

3. The computer is_____

4. The classroom is _____

5. The students are _____

6. The swirling sand is _____

7. The flood waters are _____

8. The full moon on the silent beach is _____

9. The cries of the gulls are _____

10. The soccer game is _____

Create metaphors of your own to describe the following:

11. your neighborhood

   _____

12. a rattlesnake

   _____

13. your best friend

   _____

14. sky at dawn

   _____

15. a motorcycle

   _____

Tone

Tone in a composition is the feeling that is expressed by the writer through choice of topic and through word choice throughout the paragraph or essay. The tone can be one of anger, sorrow, excitement, humor, or happiness—any emotion that the writer wants to convey.

Read each group of sentences below. Then write the tone each group of sentences expresses. Choose from the words in the box. Use each word only once.

happy	**excited**	**funny**	**worried**	**sad**

1. Wow! Today is my birthday. I know it will be a great day. We are having a chocolate cake, and we are going to play games. I can hardly wait until all my friends arrive to help me celebrate my special day.

   Tone: _____

2. I can't believe my best friend is moving away. I want to cry. Even the sky looks gray and rainy today. Nothing will ever the same again without my friend to share things with.

   Tone: _____

3. Can a pig learn tricks? My pet pig, Sally, can roll over and shake hands. Maybe I should say she can shake pig's feet. She is a funny pig who really likes to "hog the show."

   Tone: _____

4. I cannot believe that our arithmetic test is today. I forgot to study, and I do not understand multiplication. I just know I will fail this test. This could ruin my math grade. Oh, why didn't I study last night!

   Tone: _____

5. It is an absolutely beautiful day today! The sun is shining, the birds are singing, and the air smells sweet and fresh. It feels good to be alive!

   Tone: _____

Assessment: Revise and Edit a Paragraph

To revise and edit the paragraph, do the following:

♦ Put the topic sentence, supporting details, and conclusion in order.

♦ Use transition words.

♦ Add and remove details.

♦ Vary sentence structure.

♦ Correct fragments and run-on sentences.

♦ Improve word choice.

♦ Use figurative language.

Work on the paragraph on this page, and then write your final copy on the next page.

My Terrible, Horrible, Awful Day

The next thing I knew, I was on the floor beside the bed. My mother changed the sheets on my bed yesterday. I had to leave without it. When I went downstairs to the kitchen to eat breakfast. It was obvious that this day was not going to go well. I discovered there was no cereal there was no milk. I searched and searched and could not find my school backpack. I did find some stale rolls left over from the day before. The day was bad from the very beginning. They are blue with clouds on them. After such a beginning. As I woke up, I rolled over in bed. It was time to head for school. As soon as I was ready to get dressed. I went to my closet. My favorite shirt was not there. I could not even have toast. There wasn't any bread. I ate two of the rolls. It was getting late. It would be impossible for me to function at school without my backpack.

Assessment: Revise and Edit a Paragraph *(cont.)*

Write your final copy of "My Terrible, Horrible, Awful Day." You may change the title to better reflect the topic sentence. You may change the voice of the paragraph from the first person (I) to the third person (he or she) and give that person a name.

_____

_____

_____

_____

_____

_____

_____

_____

_____

_____

_____

_____

_____

Check Grammar, Capitalization, Punctuation, Spelling

After you have proofread your "Day" paragraph and have corrected all the grammar, capitalization, punctuation, and spelling, write the proofread copy below and compare it with the copy on the preceding page.

Use the checklist on the next page to review the steps you should go through each time you write a paragraph or essay. Apply the checklist each time you write.

_____

_____

_____

_____

_____

_____

_____

_____

_____

_____

_____

Paragraph Checklist

Use this checklist as part of the process whenever you write a paragraph. You should use it as a guide when you write your paragraphs for Section 6.

- ❑ Prewriting, planning, organizing
- ❑ One main idea or topic
- ❑ List of supporting details in order
- ❑ Topic sentence developed
- ❑ Supporting sentences developed
- ❑ Concluding sentence developed
- ❑ Nonessential details removed
- ❑ Supporting details added
- ❑ Varied sentence structure
- ❑ Transitions used
- ❑ Word choice improved (nouns, verbs, adjectives, adverbs)
- ❑ Similes and metaphors used
- ❑ Grammar checked
- ❑ Capitalization checked
- ❑ Punctuation checked
- ❑ Spelling checked

Descriptions of Paragraphs and Sample Topics

Expository Paragraph

Expository writing gives facts, explains ideas, or gives directions. It is nonfiction writing that informs your reader, writing that can explain how to do something. Some examples of explanatory writing are recipes, game rules, set-up instructions, machine operations, and directions. Cookbooks, diet books, textbooks, and do-it-yourself manuals are all examples of expository writing.

The following are some sample expository paragraph topics: how to ride a bike, how to write a poem, how to play your favorite sport (or any other pastime), how to sew something, how a camera works, how a hot dog is made, how to plant a garden, and how to tie knots.

Narrative Paragraph

A narrative paragraph gives the details of an experience or event in story form. It usually explains what happened in chronological order. Often the writer includes what others said and did during the experience or event, in which case, both indirect speech and direct quotations are included in the narrative. Usually, the most interesting narrative writing occurs when the writer relates an unusual or exciting experience. However, narrative writing may also be fictional.

The following are some sample narrative paragraph topics: the first time you ever did something (babysat, cooked, rode a bike); a time you were embarrassed, angry, or excited; the first or last of something (last birthday, first day of kindergarten, last vacation).

Autobiographical Paragraph

Though both expository and narrative paragraphs may be autobiographical, they are not required to be. To write an autobiographical paragraph, you must relate an episode from your own life. All of the topics listed for the narrative paragraph could be used for the autobiographical paragraph.

The following are some sample autobiographical (and narrative) paragraph topics: visits with grandparents or other relatives who live in different parts of the country or world; moving to a different city, state, or country; sharing a room with a brother/sister.

Friendly Letter

The form of a friendly letter is different, less formal, than the form used for a business letter. The heading of a friendly letter consists of three lines—two lines for the writer's address and one line for the date. The greeting is followed by a comma, and the closing is followed by a comma. The body of the letter may consist of one paragraph, especially if the letter is a "thank you," for example. Often, the body will consist of two or more paragraphs.

The content of a friendly letter should include a response to any correspondence from the person to whom you are writing; a summary of your most recent activities; any special news that you want to tell the person; and, usually, references to each other's families and any mutual friends.

Write an Expository Paragraph

Make a plan for writing a paragraph to explain how to do something, to give facts, or to give directions. Plan your paragraph.

- ◆ Choose a topic.
- ◆ Develop a topic sentence.
- ◆ Make a list of supporting details to develop into body sentences.
- ◆ Compose a concluding sentence.

topic sentence

_____

_____

list of details

_____

_____

_____

_____

_____

_____

concluding sentence

_____

_____

Write an Expository Paragraph *(cont.)*

Write the title of your paragraph on the first line, and then use your paragraph plan to write your expository paragraph.

_____

_____

_____

_____

_____

_____

_____

_____

_____

_____

_____

Write a Narrative Paragraph

Make a plan for writing about an experience or an event. Plan your paragraph.

- ◆ Choose a topic.
- ◆ Develop a topic sentence.
- ◆ Make a list of supporting details to develop into body sentences.
- ◆ Compose a concluding sentence.

topic sentence

_____

_____

list of details

_____

_____

_____

_____

_____

_____

concluding sentence

_____

_____

_____

Write a Narrative Paragraph *(cont.)*

Write the title of your paragraph on the first line and then use your paragraph plan to write your narrative paragraph.

_____

_____

_____

_____

_____

_____

_____

_____

_____

_____

_____

_____

Write an Autobiographical Paragraph

Make a plan for writing about an episode from your life. Plan your paragraph.

- ◆ Choose a topic.
- ◆ Develop a topic sentence.
- ◆ Make a list of supporting details to develop into body sentences.
- ◆ Compose a concluding sentence.

topic sentence

_____

_____

list of details

_____

_____

_____

_____

_____

concluding sentence

_____

_____

_____

Write an Autobiographical
Paragraph *(cont.)*

Write the title of your paragraph on the first line and then use your paragraph plan to write your autobiographical paragraph.

_____

_____

_____

_____

_____

_____

_____

_____

_____

_____

Write a Friendly Letter

Make a plan for writing a letter to a friend. Your friend may live nearby or far away. Plan your friendly letter.

- ◆ Respond to previous correspondence.
- ◆ Report any special news.
- ◆ Tell about your most recent activities.
- ◆ Refer to mutual friends.

response to previous correspondence

_____

_____

most recent activities

_____

_____

_____

special news

_____

_____

_____

mutual friends

_____

_____

Write a Friendly Letter *(cont.)*

Write a letter to a friend and address an envelope to send it in. Don't forget to put on a stamp before you mail it. Use the form on this page to compose your letter.

_____

_____

_____

_____

_____

_____

_____

_____

_____

_____

_____

_____

_____

Description of an Essay and Sample Topics

An essay consists of a series of paragraphs. The basic structure of the essay is the same as the structure of a paragraph:

♦ The topic sentence of the paragraph becomes an introductory paragraph.

♦ The main body sentences of the paragraph are each developed into separate paragraphs to become the body of the essay.

♦ The concluding sentence becomes a fully developed concluding paragraph.

Also, just as there are expository, narrative, comparison/contrast and persuasive paragraphs, there are expository, narrative, comparison/contrast and persuasive essays.

The following is a sample outline for a paragraph:

I. topic sentence—I would like very much to have my very own dog.

II. supporting details—There are three reasons I think I should have my own dog.

  A. first reason—The one dog we have seems to belong more to my older brother.

  B. second reason—Both of us cannot go to different places with Buster at the same time.

  C. third reason—I think that it is just as important for me to have a pet that is my companion as it is for my brother to have one.

III. concluding sentence—For these reasons, I think that I should be allowed to have a dog.

This paragraph outline can easily be expanded into an outline for an essay. Each supporting detail can be developed into a paragraph by giving more details about it and by using examples. On the next page is an expansion of the above paragraph outline into an essay outline.

Description of an Essay and Sample Topics *(cont.)*

The following is an example of an outline of an essay:

I. **Introduction**—I would like very much to have my very own dog.

   A. The dog we have now came into our family before I was born.

   B. Buster was friends with my older brother before he ever knew me.

II. **Body**—There are three reasons I think I should have my own dog.

   A. Buster seems to belong to my older brother.

      1. He always goes to Jerry first.

      2. If my brother starts to leave the house, Buster always wants to go with him.

   B. Both of us cannot go to different places at the same time with Buster.

      1. It seems that every time I want to take Buster with me for a walk, Jerry has already left to take Buster somewhere else.

      2. When I am home alone, I would like to have a dog who is loyal to only me.

   C. I think it is just as important for me to have a pet as it is for Jerry to have one.

      1. Just as Jerry has, I can learn to be responsible for a pet.

      2. Just as Jerry has his, I could have my own loyal companion.

III. **Conclusion**—Therefore, I think it would be a good idea for me to have my own dog.

   A. I would have a pet to care for and one to care for me.

   B. The dog would get to know me from the beginning and be my loyal companion.

In addition to using the same kinds of topics for expository and narrative essays as for expository and narrative paragraphs, you can also write both comparison-contrast and persuasive-opinion paragraphs and essays.

☞ For a *comparison/contrast* paragraph or essay, you write about what common characteristics someone or something shares and then about those things that are very different about someone or something.

☞ For a *persuasive* paragraph or essay, you write about what you think about someone or something and try to convince your readers to agree with you by giving good reasons, examples, and evidence to support your position.

Choose an Essay Topic and List Ideas

You may write about any topic you choose, and you may write any kind of essay you choose.

That means you may write an expository essay in which you explain how to do something. You may write a narrative essay in which you tell a story about some event in your life. You may write an essay in which you give your opinions about a subject and try to persuade your reader to agree with you. You may write a comparison/contrast essay pointing out the similarities and differences between two people or things.

Choose a topic for your essay.

Topic _____

Write down all the ideas you can think of that you could use to develop and support your topic. Think of examples, incidents, reasons—all the details that you could possibly use to support your essay topic.

List your ideas: _____

_____

_____

_____

_____

_____

_____

_____

_____

Essay Outline

Use the outline on page 39 and the form below as guides for writing an outline for your essay.

I. _____

    A. _____

    B. _____

II. _____

    A. _____

        1. _____

        2. _____

    B. _____

        1. _____

        2. _____

    C. _____

        1. _____

        2. _____

III. _____

    A. _____

    B. _____

Develop Essay Paragraphs

Use your outline from the previous page to develop the five paragraphs of your essay.

Introduction (I. A. B.)

_____

_____

_____

_____

_____

Body Paragraph II A. (II. A. 1. 2.)

_____

_____

_____

_____

_____

_____

_____

Develop Essay Paragraphs *(cont.)*

Body Paragraph II. B. (II. B. 1. 2.)

_____

_____

_____

_____

_____

_____

_____

Body Paragraph II. C. (II. C. 1. 2.)

_____

_____

_____

_____

_____

_____

_____

Develop Essay Paragraphs *(cont.)*

Conclusion (III. A. B.)

_____

_____

_____

_____

_____

_____

_____

_____

_____

_____

Decide on a title for your essay. Remember that it should reflect what you write in your introduction so that your reader knows what the subject of the essay is.

Essay Title: _____

Revise, Edit, and Proofread the Essay

Use the following checklist to revise, edit, and proofread your essay. Then, write and proofread the final copy of your essay.

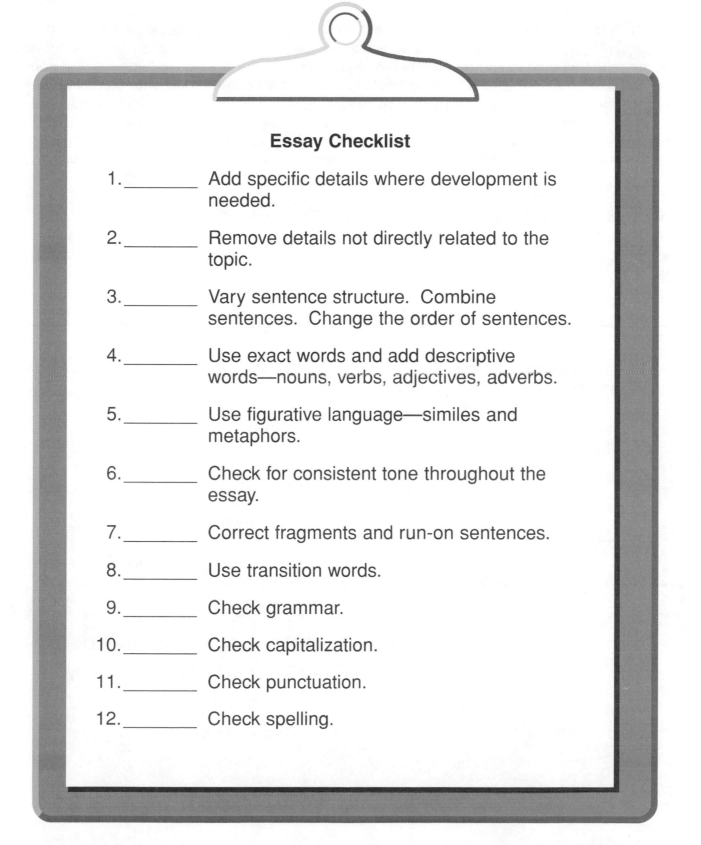

Essay Checklist

1. _____ Add specific details where development is needed.

2. _____ Remove details not directly related to the topic.

3. _____ Vary sentence structure. Combine sentences. Change the order of sentences.

4. _____ Use exact words and add descriptive words—nouns, verbs, adjectives, adverbs.

5. _____ Use figurative language—similes and metaphors.

6. _____ Check for consistent tone throughout the essay.

7. _____ Correct fragments and run-on sentences.

8. _____ Use transition words.

9. _____ Check grammar.

10. _____ Check capitalization.

11. _____ Check punctuation.

12. _____ Check spelling.

Unit Assessment

Read the paragraph and answer the questions that follow it. Fill in the circles beside the correct answers.

Ricky, Good Friend

(1) Ricky, the dog who became my best friend, just mysteriously appeared at our house one day. (2) My mother said that his appearance was not really mysterious. (3) She thought that someone who no longer wanted him dropped him off near our house because that person knew we like dogs. (4) Because no one else in the family seemed much interested in him, I decided that Ricky was mine and that I would name him. (5) I named him Ricky because I was watching on television a singer I admired named Ricky when Dog Ricky appeared in our front yard. (6) Why anyone would not want to keep Ricky I could not understand, for he was a loving dog and a mild-mannered one if he did not think he was protecting me from villains. (7) It is true that I always felt safe when Ricky was around. (8) With him to protect me, I did not mind being home alone. (9) Also, I could always count on Ricky to be sympathetic if I thought someone had treated me unfairly or if I had suffered a disappointment of any kind. (10) His understanding eyes helped soothe my bruised heart every time. (11) Even when he became old and slow and his vision blurred, Ricky always came to my defense like a fierce tiger. (12) For my money, he had the best qualities a pet should have: Ricky was loyal and loving.

---

1. Which of these words is used as a transition?

   ⓐ I

   ⓑ Why

   ⓒ Also

   ⓓ Oh

   ⓔ none of these

2. Which is the topic sentence?

   ⓐ 12

   ⓑ 6

   ⓒ 5

   ⓓ 2

   ⓔ none of these

3. Which is the concluding sentence?

   ⓐ 1

   ⓑ 11

   ⓒ 10

   ⓓ 9

   ⓔ none of these

4. Which supporting details did the writer have on her list?

   ⓐ appearance, name, safe, sympathy

   ⓑ mystery, name, old, barking

   ⓒ Mother, family, villains, money

   ⓓ Ricky, singer, safe, eyes, food

   ⓔ none of these

5. In addition to the word "Ricky," what other word is used throughout the paragraph to support the main idea?

   (a) person
   (b) sense
   (c) protecting
   (d) count
   (e) none of these

6. How many body sentences are there?

   (a) 10
   (b) 12
   (c) 11
   (d) 9
   (e) none of these

7. Which expression is a simile?

   (a) "I could count on him"
   (b) "mysteriously appeared"
   (c) "like a fierce tiger"
   (d) "His understanding eyes"
   (e) none of these

8. Which kind of paragraph is this?

   (a) narrative
   (b) expository
   (c) comparison
   (d) persuasive
   (e) none of these

9. Which of these words is used as an adjective to describe the pronoun "one" in sentence 6?

   (a) mild-mannered
   (b) loyal
   (c) loving
   (d) understanding
   (e) none of these

10. Which of these words is used as an adverb to describe the verb "came" in sentence 10?

   (a) mysteriously
   (b) really
   (c) much
   (d) always
   (e) none of these

11. Which of these words is used as a conjunction in sentence 6?

   (a) for
   (b) just
   (c) anyone
   (d) not
   (e) none of these

12. Which sentence has words in a series separated by commas?

   (a) 1
   (b) 4
   (c) 6
   (d) 10
   (e) none of these

13. Which of these sentences could be safely removed from the paragraph ?

   (a) 2
   (b) 8
   (c) 11
   (d) 1
   (e) none of these

14. Which of these titles could also be used for this paragraph?

   (a) My Dog Spot
   (b) Safe from Villains
   (c) My Heart Beats for Ricky
   (d) A Loyal and Loving Pet
   (e) none of these

Answer Key

Page 5

1. The, Eiffel, Tower, Paris, France
2. Edgar, Allan, Poe, The, Fall, House, Usher
3. The, The, Castle, Attic, Middle, Ages
4. I, Car, Driver, Tuesday, March
5. The, Statue, Liberty, United, States, France, New, York, City
6. Did, Thanksgiving, Day, Fifth, Avenue
7. The, Taj, Mahal, Indian, Hindu, Muslim
8. The, Nutcracker, Christmas,
9. I, Dr., Hutchison, I, Oakwood, Hospital, Best, Texas

Page 6

1. "Please give our guest a warm welcome," said the host of the talk show.
2. "Governor, how will the new tax increase affect the local schools?" asked the reporter.
3. "Be careful driving to work," warned the meteorologist. "Freezing temperatures have caused black ice to form on the highways."
4. Mars, Jupiter, Venus, and Saturn are planets in our solar system.
5. The baby's tears wouldn't stop for hours.
6. The *Titanic* sank in the Atlantic Ocean on April 15, 1912, and there were relatively few survivors of that awful night.
7. Flour, eggs, and cheese are on the shopping list, but I don't know when I'm going to the store.

Page 7

1. Where
2. There, eight
3. toe
4. grown
5. Would
6. Too, sea
7. role, witch
8. hear, planes
9. road, steel
10. know, sew
11. fourth-grade, trip, to, there
12. everyone, groups, tour, blue, group, see, bears, red
13. group, seals, yellow, group, walked, monkey, noon
14. groups, lunch, ate, sandwiches, water, After, lunch
15. bird, theater, over, time

Page 9

   I went to the store because I needed to get something for lunch. My stomach was growling so much that a little boy sitting in a shopping cart could hear it. "Mom," he said, "he has a rumbly tumbly." "Shush," said his mother. I turned to the little boy and asked, "I have a what?" "A rumbly tumbly," he said and smiled shyly. "A rumbly tumbly, a rumbly tumbly," I said over and over again. The little boy started to giggle, and I was even hungrier than before. "Yikes!" I said to the little boy. "I have to get something to eat before my rumbly tumbly tumbles." The little boy stopped giggling, pointed his finger at me, and said, "Go get something to eat right now before your rumbly tumbly tumbles." "Okay," I said, as I rushed down the aisle toward the apples and bananas.

Page 10

1. Thanksgiving
2. movies
3. wintertime
4. good friend
5. exercise
6. pets

Page 12

3-9-1-5-4-7-8-2-6

Page 18

I got a good grade on my last homework assignment, though.
Last week at school I had hall duty.
Our home fireplace uses gas.
I can't remember whether I put plenty of food in my fish tank at home.
My mother says that the fish at our local market do not always seem fresh to her.

Page 24

1. excited
2. sad
3. funny
4. worried
5. happy

Pages 46 and 47

1. c
2. e
3. b
4. a
5. e
6. d
7. c
8. a
9. a
10. d
11. a
12. e
13. b
14. d